# Souvenirs

poems by A.D. Owens

*for the ones who stay up all night creating art.*
*we never get enough sleep.*

# contents

saudade

I.

ever so blue.
ever so mine.
ever so lovely
when our hands intertwine.

## II.

you
    were,
        are,
           and will be
               my favorite thing
                    for miles.

III.

I heard a rumor
and it didn't go away.

is a rumor really a rumor
if it's still here to stay?

IV.

please don't go
if I ask you to stay.

I just want to pretend
another day.

V.

tell me a story
so I can feel.

tell me a story
make it seem real.

tell me a story
so I can endear.

tell me anything
before I disappear.

## VI.

show me
the flowers.

show me
your soul.

show me
your scars,
new and old.

show me
you won't fade
when something
new shows.

show me
you love me
more than control.

show me
that money
isn't what
you'd rather hold.

VII.

I fell for a frog
when I wanted a prince.

I fell for a smile
and let the devil in.

VIII.

it's a sick feeling when you're not around,
I spend hours lying on the ground.

I play your records on repeat,
listening to one song each day
that seems to get me.

I wear your t-shirt, so I won't feel lonely.
I bought a PlayStation, so time would move less slowly.

does it get lonely up in Norway?
should I come up your way?

should I pay the price to see you
instead of losing you
and just dance the night away?

tkm
boy pablo

IX.

wine, oh wine,
please save me.

I'm stuck in a place
where sleep is a disgrace.

where time ticks slowly,
and the thing I wanted
was stolen.

it happens every day.

X.

I'm addicted to you,
belladonna.

it should be criminal,
belladonna.

the way you have me roped in,
and every move is a sin.

will you cut me loose?
or do I have to escape to win,
belladonna?

## XI.

he's just a phantom lover
who's found another
to discover
in the few months of summer.

she's just a stunner
who's found another
to play a lover
before she takes everything but the plunger.

XII.

I aim and fire,
miss the canvas by a mile.

leaves my mind in a blank state,
makes me kick over a can of paint.

but then I hear a whisper
that makes me feel anew,

it makes me pick up a paintbrush and uncover
that I'm a sucker for some luster,
but never good at getting gold.

that I'm searching for love in all the wrong places,
searching for love to fill blank spaces,
and now it's getting old.

friends, foes, and everything in
between

XIII.

I spilled my soul across blank pages
hoping that it could somehow erase you.

it only made me see the good in you
until I recounted the scars.

I'll never understand
how we took things that far.

XIV.

I don't want
to fix what was broken.

I don't want
to talk to you.

I don't want
to answer your questions.

because if I do,

I'll miss you
    love you
    hate you
    and want you

all
    over
        again.

XV.

here I am
taken by surprise.

you said the right things,
you didn't tell lies.

I don't know
if I'll trust you again.

I don't know
if it's worth it in the end.

XVI.

you only wanted my body,
I wanted to give you my heart.

you only wanted my body,
I decided we should part.

XVII.

the signs
were all there,

but I was full
of despair.

I walked
blind

to feel
something

I thought
would be divine,

but you
were you

and I was
set adrift.

you left me
emptier

than my person
before,

I take
the blame

for expecting
you

to be more.

how could you
be more
with your issues?

how could you
be more

when you take frequent
walks
in the past
because you miss it?

it's why
you grasp at straws
to hold it all

like you're waiting
for the fall
in the present.

it's why
you never really try,

just promise
enough times,

to keep
us close

but inconsistent.

XVIII.

sometimes,
the toughest things
are those unanswered questions

swimming in our minds
that usually start with "why?"

they embody the ones
who become unforgettable
to our inner child.

XIX.

real friends
don't disappear.

they don't only text you
on new year's.

real friends
don't bleed you dry,

then come back
next week
around the same time.

real friends
aren't Superman.

they won't
save you at every fall,

but their support
says it all.

they're there
when the world's
closing in

and you won't have
to question,

are they a friend?

XX.

if my eyes were closed,
I would know if you were around.

you always smelled like tobacco
and peppermint so profound.

I told you my secrets
and you told me your past.

I was drawn to you because
of all the things you had.

you had the car.
   you had the house.
      you had the money.
         you had the wardrobe.
        you had dogs.
           you had the tats.
              you had children.
                you had the career.
                    you had it all except love.

I once caught you outside
in the drizzling rain,

I think you were smoking
to remove the pain.

I asked you for one
and you told me no.

I asked for a favor later
and you became a ghost.

XXI.

you're a puppet on strings
dancing for your life

until the strings are cut
or you break inside.

you weren't careful
with your words
and now the people talk.

your demons burned a hole
in your pocket, leaving a mark.

I don't think you're sorry
for what you did,
only sorry you got caught.

I hope I'm wrong.
I hope you've changed a lot.

I hope you fixed the hate
and it isn't all talk.

don't let the devil
catch you twice,

he doesn't make promises
that you'll go unscathed.

XXII.

I wonder
if we got to your head

and the drive is
now dead

because you're not a nobody
anymore.

did your expectations
disappear?

or did you bake away
your fears?

because who
wants to feel

when they
take and take

the pieces
they want of you

to put you
up there.

XXIII.

he's just a phase,
don't you know?

a warm body to touch
while the winter winds blow.

he was trouble from the start,
but you didn't care
you wanted his body—
not his heart.

brown-eyed girl,
don't you know?

he's just a phase
until the snow decides
it doesn't want to snow.

he's the one
so christmas won't be lonely.

he's the one
that makes you feel like you're talking to nobody.

brown-eyed girl,
don't you know?

your new year's kiss
was just for show.

so no one would think
you were alone.

so no one would know
you feel unknown.

brown-eyed girl,
I think you know,

that it's time
for him to go.

I hope I don't see
him for a while.

I hope you'll forget
his good-looking smile.

brown-eyed girl
from across the way,

delete his number
so you won't be tempted
to ever answer
his "hey."

XXIV.

you were the boy
who lost his shoes,

who sat in the corner
and sang the blues.

you watched me dance
with another man,

it didn't bother you
when we kissed and he held my hands.

if you were even a little jealous,
would you have asked me to dance?

would we have been more than two strangers
who text every now and then?

now you're full of confidence over the phone,
is it because we talk like good friends?

or is it something more?

XXV.

I struck a match
and set fire to our little shed.

I sat in the grass
and watched it burn

with saddened eyes

as the flames
climbed,

and the smoke
made its way to the clouds.

I struck a match
and you decided to come by,

I wasn't sure why

because you
liked us underground.

you tried to
fight me

instead of
the fire,

and that's
when I knew

I did the
right thing.

while you
threw things
all around me,

I dreamt
a better you.

XXVI.

I didn't like you
the moment we met.

it was the way
you constantly tapped
your foot on my chair

even after
I told you to quit.

but it wasn't
just my chair,

it was my shoulder
too.

you always asked
me questions

even though
your friends
were right next you.

I'm not sure
what it was,

but I eventually saw
you were one of the
good ones.

could you thank your
brother for me?

he gave me the 411.

XXVII.

I met a beautiful girl
who acted like a child.

she was bubbly and young,
bashful but sly.

nicotine was her poison,
but she craved boys.

she had a few kisses
and forbidden touches,
but she wanted more.

I never quite understood
what went on in that head of hers.

I think I just met a teenage girl.

XXVIII.

you were loud and wild
when I met you.

the way you drove,
the way you talked,

the way you laughed
when it was hard to stop.

calculus made you angry,
so you'd FaceTime me a lot.

I'll never forget you
because you did the sweetest thing.

showing up at my door
with ice cream and candy,

when you knew I needed
someone to hear me.

I hate that you
don't pick up the phone,

but I know you
still support me.

don't chase your dreams
Naseem,

attract them.

XXIX.

I know a girl
with the brightest smile.

she falls for boys
for a minute or awhile.

she lets them into her heart.

she lets them in thinking
they won't part.

she escapes the world
until she feels healed.

she escapes the world
not knowing what's real.

when she comes back,
and she always does,

she realizes the world
left her in the dust.

I know a girl
with the brightest smile,

who met an ex,
who had regrets,

and now they're expecting
their first child.

XXX.

I know a girl
who loves Chanel.

she loves the feel
of a designer heel.

her heart was set on
being a wedding planner.

her brain realized
she made more taking care
of those to be buried.

I know a girl
who loves Chanel.

she likes pink things
and gourmet meals.

death doesn't faze her,
it pays the bills.

it lets her buy Vogue.
it lets her set sail.
it lets her buy seven rings
just for thrills.

I know a girl
who loves Chanel.

XXXI.

dear sweet, innocent girl,
I wish I could be you.

your mind is wild and free,
and you don't give boys
any of your time.

you blush at the thought of romance.
you don't think you'll ever marry,
even if given the chance.

you're happy
when you're alone.

you're happy
with your friends.

you're happy
working hard to be a career girl
until the very end.

dear sweet, innocent girl,
stay true to you.

your purity is surreal
in a world so dark and cruel.

XXXII.

pretty one
with her head above the clouds,

don't let their thoughts
start to bring you down.

they know not what they do,
they do not realize your love
to them is true.

cherish the one
who holds you in his arms,

who wants to tell the world,
till death do us part.

pretty one
who works so hard
night and day,

let your worries fade
and your troubles be at bay.

## XXXIII.

baker boy
baker boy,
now is the time.

baker boy
baker boy,
you're on the rise.

baker boy
baker boy,
dream so big.

baker boy
baker boy,
take a swig.

XXXIV.

you had
no name
to me when you
were alive.

no name
to me when you
died.

I did
think about you
a few times.

miserly,
selfishly,

not about
your memory.

I didn't have
memories with you.

I don't regret
it too.

I just can't
come to terms
with why
it was your time.

I don't think
I'll ever really will.

faith and family

XXXV.

I often wait for a sign from God
that the world can be a good place.

it never comes when I ask for it.

XXXVI.

do I believe
because
this is what I hold true?

or do I believe
because
I'm told to?

## XXXVII.

have you met Sunday?
she's quite divine.

she sees lots of people
sitting in lines.

bowing heads
giving tithes,

stuffing faces
spreading lies,

leaving early
before its time.

posing as believers
of the lord of light.

posing as believers
for the person
to their right.

have you met Sunday?
she's quite divine.

most of her brothers and sisters
only visit a few times.

## XXXVIII.

merry christmas
to the ones who are gone,
the ones who fill my heart with song.

I light a candle for you,
then I light one for peace on earth.

XXXIX.

I wrote these words
for you
the only son.

blood of woman,
strength of God.

I envy the purity you have
and I lost.

the blood on my hands
that wasn't of another.

the blood on my hands
that was my own,
don't tell my mother.

I'm far from perfect,
tell our father.

tell him
that we're a billion souls in his sea,

that we're just broken organs
trying to find a tune,

like shepherds roaming
the earth under the moon.

I'm still learning,
tell the spirit.

tell it
that it touched my soul.

that it helped me heal in the dark.

that I'm thankful it helped me
feel something bigger than myself.

for you
the only son,
the better half of mankind.

your shoes can't be filled,
but I hope I make a difference
the way that you did.

I desire to want less
and love more

to let patience lead me
ashore.

to die leaving nothing
unsaid

and no stone
unturned.

XL.

I like lemonade in the rain.
it's the sweet thing that takes away the pain.

I have a catalogue of afternoons in my head
that remind me of all the good times we spent.

my favorite memory was us setting up your tent.
so we could see shooting stars and stare upon the moon.

it's hard to forget the damage you made,
when you decided to put a bullet in your frame.

I wish I could reach you so I could hold your hand.
I wish I could reach you so I could understand.

so you could tell me why,
so these tears could finally dry.

I like lemonade in the rain.
it's the sweet thing that takes away the pain,

like the anniversary of your death,
no one could seem to explain.

XLI.

when I was a little girl,
I thought you were scary.

I saw sagging lines
and sunken eyes,
and it made me afraid
to go near you,

when I was supposed to
hug you and love you.

it used to make you mad,
it gave Dad a good laugh.

when I was in middle school,
I realized why you looked that way.

I felt ashamed.

but you were gone
and I couldn't apologize at all.

I used to beat myself up
all the time,

because I thought you
died thinking

I didn't love you.

## XLII.

when I was little,
we danced together.

you said it was practice
for my wedding.

now I am older,
and life seems fast.

but I'd rather be
your little girl,

who danced with you
in the center of a room,

who had no rhythm,
who accidentally
stepped on your shoes.

I'd rather be
right next to you,

the one who makes me laugh,
and made me fall in love with jazz.

I love you.

XLIII.

I once had an argument
with my mother
over a cake.

"the frosting
has too much butter,"
she said.

"it isn't the right
ratio to sugar,"
she said.

I had nothing to say
for the rest of the night.

the next day she apologized
and a wrong was made right.

we laughed about it in the kitchen,
while my sister spilled the tea
over the phone to our grandmother.

XLIV.

I asked my parents for a treehouse,
they quickly said no.

they said, "ask your grandparents,
that's what we did a long time ago."

I asked my grandparents for a treehouse,
they quickly laughed.

they said "we're too old for such a task,
our bones would surely crack."

I stopped asking for a treehouse
knowing my wish wouldn't come true.

instead, I took my cousins
and my sister outside
where the sky was blue,

where the sunshine gleamed
and the mulberry tree leaned.

where the strawberries were sweet
and our mud pies weren't so neat.

where we climbed in the big oak,
where the frisbee would sail,

before finishing the day playing tag,
and jumping over the chain fence rail.

sometimes I wish I had a treehouse,
I cannot lie.

but I treasure more
the time between
cousins, sister, and I.

prescriptions to myself

XLV.

it's been a while,
but you've been here before.

I know you don't want to face it,
but it'll happen more and more.

it's okay to cry,
know you won't be forever blue.

it's only goodbye for now,
you'll see them soon.

when you're ready,
leave the tears behind,
let your smile arise.

they'll send you a sign
that they're okay.

it'll be okay.

one day the pain will be gone
and you'll only remember,

remember who they were
and who they were to you.

XLVI.

be brave enough
to do the things you love.

be wise enough
to know when to let go.

be kind enough
because you might touch
someone else's soul.

XLVII.

love
will find you,

don't you worry
your pretty little heart.

set your mind
on things above.

keep on loving you,
dove.

when you least
expect it,

love will come.

XLVIII.

loving is easy.
life is hard.

it's the little things
that try to tear us apart.

loving is easy.
being human is hard.

it's okay to take a night off
and do whatever you bloody want.

loving is easy.
trust is hard.

guard your heart carefully,
because cruel intentions
don't only hide in the dark.

loving is easy.
desires are hard.

sometimes the prettiest things
are only the prettiest in your head.

loving is easy.
loving yourself can be hard.

learn to love what you see
before you seek love from another heart.

XLIX.

just because you feel broken,
doesn't mean life won't get better again.

just because you're hurt,
isn't a reason to punish everyone else.

just because you listened,
doesn't mean you owe them any more of your time.

just because they apologized,
doesn't mean you have to let them back into your life.

L.

don't say, "I'm fine,"
when you really aren't.

don't say, "yes"
to everything,

and let people take
advantage of your big heart.

don't be ashamed
that you made mistakes.

don't stand by
and let ignorance take place.

do tell your truth
and know not everyone
will agree with it,

and that's okay.

LI.

I don't care what "they" say.

you never
need a reason

to trust
to love
to be proud of you.

LII.

life
is never still.

so dance
in every color
you feel.

LIII.

it's lonely
on the other side
of the room,

watching a party
with no one
watching you.

the darkness
whispers lies

and you struggle
to cut ties

because there's a party
on the other side
of the room.

where light makes
everything shine

and you can drown
your thoughts
in rye,

just like you're
suppose to.

it's lonely
on the other side
of the room.

you can drown
in your head

but if you
make it out instead,

kudos to you.

LIV.

right now
you're on the ground,

strumming your guitar
to the music in your ears

that makes you feel
safe and sound.

it's okay
to take some
time for yourself,

but don't forget
the time
you spend on
one thing

takes away
from
everything
else.

LV.

a blank page isn't your enemy,
a blank page is your friend.

the friend who doesn't mind
if you keep them up all night.

the friend who lets you make
mistakes again and again.

the friend you can spill wine on
and won't get angry

—unless it's your laptop.

please for the love of everything good,
do not spill wine on your laptop.

daydreams and other things

LVI.

fall, winter, summer, spring,
look at all the things you bring.

one brings leaves,
one brings snow,
one brings flowers,

and one makes me
want lots of showers.

LVII.

dear Dr. Seuss,
your rhymes were stuck
in my head.

it was that Netflix show,
*Green Eggs and Ham.*

LVIII.

the best view is up in the sky,
it's where you can kiss reality goodbye.

no one can bother you for miles,
and the clouds give you a reason to smile.

I like the tiny little houses and dot-sized cars.
I like that I can't even see people anymore.

I always feel like I'm traveling to another world,
where good things are always in store.

## LIX.

when music fills my ears
and sunshine touches my skin,

I feel ready to return to my life
and the world once again.

LX.

there's a song I know
that when I close my eyes,
I'm transported to my paradise.

I can see myself sitting in a chair
with sunglasses on
and sunshine warming my hair.

I can feel the sand between my toes
making my skin soft,
making me glow.

I can hear the waves crashing on the beach
beckoning me to come,
beckoning me to reach,

beckoning me to feel something
that might make me complete.

I can taste the salt of the ocean
after the wave I ride
knocks me over.

there's a song I know
that when I close my eyes,
I'm transported to my paradise.

and even though it isn't real,
someday I'll be back
and the memories will hold still.

LXI.

sometimes,
I feel like I have to cry.

not because I'm sad,
not because I'm blue.

I just need to feel
another emotion
or two.

life in quarantine

LXII.

if I died tomorrow,
would you care?

or

would I be
a forgotten body

six feet under

beside strangers
from ear-to-ear?

LXIII.

every day is starting
to seem the same.

Mondays are Fridays
and Fridays are Sundays.

time never moved
more slowly.

learning about the world
from a glowing box,

learning that people know
less than they thought.

looking at life
through a pane of glass,

wondering when I will
be free at last.

so I can stop spending
half my time in bed,

so I can stop living
in my head,

so I can see something
or someone new instead.

I miss people.

LXIV.

some fear God
who could strike them dead.

some fear writers
who can make their mistakes
live long after they're dead.

LXV.

you're blind if you don't see
we live in a fake world,

where money is enough to
make someone fall on their sword,

where narratives are painted
to sway your thinking,

where we strongly take a stand
until the interest is shrinking.

why do the issues that divide us
have to be trending to be noticed?

why do businesses feel the need
to tell the world how much money
they donated?

is it just business?
do they want some attention?
a pat on the back?

or are they afraid
if they don't say,

people will drag them
and not think twice?

this world is so fake,
it's tragic.

everyone is as real
as plastic.

cancel her,
not him.

support this,
not that.

you brought this here,
go back.

why is it so hard
for all of us to get along?

why do we hide
behind tweets
from fake profiles?

all I see is toxicity
in these stans,

saying you're all about love
and posting hate

in the name of an idol
you've never even met.

when did criticizing
become animosity?

when did we forget about the art
and care about the streams?

why are we out for blood
over the littlest things?

why?

why aren't we better
than this?

LXVI.

american roads
have a strange color.

blood in the gravel,
blood in the stone,

blood from black bodies
lying on the road.

frame by frame
we replay them
losing their breath

from the evil among us
that taints the rest.

red is
what I see,
what I feel,
what hurts.

red is
what's spilling from fruit
so dark and lovely,
so sweet with deep roots.

fruit that is
not immune to gunshots,
not immune to abuse,
not immune to brutality,
just like you.

so, don't forget.

don't forget
what you've seen.

because when we do,

the outrage the world
is voicing—

folds.

the important conversations
and the needed changes—

stop.

but the blood
doesn't.

evil
doesn't.

racism
doesn't
stop.

LXVII.

poetry reads like a diary
you weren't supposed to touch.

itching to know what's inside,
but you didn't have to
because it was unlocked.

you had permission
to be so close
to my thoughts.

to read them
again and again,
until you wanted to stop.

to show someone
else if you wanted to or not.

you're so close
that you might
as well be
in my head,

that you might
pretend we're friends,

but we're not.

www.ingramcontent.com/pod-product-compliance
Lightning Source LLC
Chambersburg PA
CBHW021136020426
42331CB00005B/795